QUICK & EASY
decorative
painting

QUICK & EASY
decorative
painting

Peggy Jessee

NORTH LIGHT BOOKS
CINCINNATI, OHIO
www.nlbooks.com

About the Author

I started decorative painting in the late 70s when I took a five day seminar from Priscilla Hauser. Decorative painting has been a part of my life ever since. I have been privileged enough to take classes from some of the best teachers and artists in the industry. I consider myself lucky to have found what I love to do and even luckier to be able to share it with you through this book. I love to teach painting classes and will continue to teach at the Heart of Ohio Tole Convention in Columbus and in my home studio.

I live in Cincinnati, Ohio with my husband Ray and my daughter, Angie and her husband Bob, who have given me the greatest love in life, besides painting, and that is my wonderful grandsons, Jacob and Zachary.

Other fine North Light books are available from your local bookstore, art supply store or direct from the publisher.

04 03 02 01 00   5 4 3 2

Library of Congress Cataloging-in-Publication Data

Jessee, Peggy
    Quick & Easy Decorative Painting / Peggy Jessee
       p.   cm.
   ISBN 0-89134-990-1 (pbk. : alk. paper)
   1. Painting 2. Decoration and ornament--Plant forms. I. Title: Quick and Easy Decorative Painting. II. Title.
TT385.J47 2000
745.7'23--dc21

Editor: Heather Dakota
Designer: Mary Barnes-Clark
Cover Design: Amber Traven
Photography: Christine Polomsky
Production Coordinator: Sara Dumford

Dedication

I want to dedicate this book to my parents, Bruce Richardson and the late Evie Richardson, for being the most important thing in life, "good parents."

Acknowledgments

Whenever you are given the opportunity to do a project such as this there are a lot of people to thank, but you may never get them all thanked properly.

First and foremost, thanks to my husband Ray for putting up with the extra "mess" and for helping to make sure I had the time I needed for projects, photo shoots and meetings.

Thanks to the people at North Light, Kathy Kipp and Heather Dakota, who had faith in me, even though I thought you were crazy for approaching *me* for this book. I also want to thank Christine Polomsky, a great photographer who took the fear out of photo shoots. You are all wonderful people to work with. Thanks also to Mary Barnes-Clark and Amber Traven for the beautiful and fun design for this book. You made my work look great!

I especially want to thank The Society of Decorative Painters, an organization I have been a part of since I began painting with Priscilla Hauser more years ago than I can believe. Because of the work of the society members, it is possible for people like me to learn from the best in the decorative painting field at seminars and conventions. If you like to paint the Society has a place for you to learn and grow.

I also want to thank my painting and traveling buddies, Valerie Bernardino and Jude Creager, for the good times as we travel to conventions and learn more about our Decorative Art.

I want most to thank God for all my blessings.

Table of Contents

Color Chart: Yellows

Butter Yellow

Straw

Golden Brown

Dark Goldenrod

Antique Gold

Crocus Yellow

Calypso Orange

Introduction

Welcome to *Quick & Easy Decorative Painting*. You'll find that by practicing your brushstrokes you'll be able to decorate everything from coasters to furniture pieces with designs that are truly your own.

There are many ways to paint flowers, fruit and foliage that can take a long time, but as I tell my students—I am the Queen of "Instant Gratification." I like to see progress in a short time.

When I start a project, I don't have a clue what it will look like when I am finished. I start by selecting the flower or fruit that will be my focal point and I build from there. I select the area where I want the focal point, and paint around that fruit or flower. I love painting freehand because tracing is time consuming. However, don't feel you have to do the same. Use the patterns included in this book, but with practice you'll soon be painting without patterns, too.

My rules for painting are simple:

1. Play with color combinations to find the colors you *love*.

2. Practice and enjoy your time painting. I believe,

"If you paint what you love, and with the colors you love, you'll love what you paint."

-Peggy Jessee

Where do you get those ideas?

There are a lot of places to look for design ideas and color schemes. Look at greeting cards, especially when you travel. Check out the local gift shops for cards and wrapping paper from small companies. They have beautiful art work. I often find a flower in a design or just a color combination I like, so I buy the card to add to my "idea book."

Look at the bargain books in bookstores. I have found several gardening books with fantastic pictures of flowers and fruit that give me ideas for easy designs. For example, while doing this book, I found a picture of "Johnny-jump-ups" and realized the flowers could be painted with a few basic strokes and a little line work.

Don't forget to look at seed packets and seed catalogs for ideas, especially for color and flower details. When I find pictures in catalogs or magazines I cut them out for my "idea book." And remember to take your camera wherever you go. Your photographs will make a nice addition to your "idea book," too.

What is an "Idea Book"?

I use a sketch book I purchased at a local craft supplier. It has a heavy cover so it won't get bent. Some books have plain paper and some have a few lines for notes. I tape or glue my magazine pictures or photos on the pages, and make a few notes about colors or designs to use at a later time. I often go to department stores and look at the bath towels on display. I find this an easy way to visualize color combinations. Seeing different solid colors together helps me plan color schemes and gives me a lot of ideas. Fabric stores are another great place to look for color combinations.

I also love to go through the silk flowers at craft stores. I often buy a single stem of flowers and keep all my finds in a huge container in my studio for inspiration. Once, when I was purchasing a sprig of flowers at my local craft store a clerk told me, "God never made that flower in that color." My reply was ". . . but, God made all the colors."

Practice, play and most of all, have fun. You'll be surprised at the wonderful color combinations you discover and how creative you can be.

What You'll Need

General Supplies

Brush Basin: A good brush basin has two or three compartments for water and grooves for brushes to rest on without touching the sides or bottom of the container. Brush basins usually have a set of ridges to rub the bristles over to help remove paint. To avoid damaging your brushes, never jam them on the ridges, but rub gently.

Sandpaper: Most of the wood pieces in craft stores today are very good and need only light sanding with a no. 220 grit sandpaper. I usually use the sanding pads purchased in craft, hardware and paint stores. They are more expensive than regular sandpaper, but last a long time and usually have a different grit on each side, some are very rough and some are very fine. Check out the variety and you'll find what works best for you.

Tack Rag: Tack rags are usually cheesecloth that has been soaked in a liquid (usually varnish) then dried to a tacky feel. Tack rags are used to remove sanding dust from your wood surface. Store your tack rag in an airtight container to keep it sticky. A Ziploc bag or a glass jar with a lid works fine.

Palette: There are many types of palettes. You'll find paper palettes at your local art supply store. Make sure they are suitable for acrylic paint. Styrofoam plates, glazed ceramic tile or metal pans can also be used.

Paper Towels: I like to use soft paper towels to clean my brushes, so as not to cause damage to the bristles. It is important that the paper towel not leave lint. It will get into your paint.

Wood Sealer: I recommend a water-based wood sealer, so you can mix

your sealer with your basecoat color. There are many good sealers on the market: Delta's wood sealer, Jo Sonja's All Purpose sealer or J.W. Etc. wood sealers are all great.

Varnish: If you start reading the labels on varnish cans, it will drive you crazy. There are so many from which to choose—oil-based, water-based, acrylic or polymer. Stick with a water-based product. My favorites are Delta and J.W. Etc. Right-Step Varnish. Most varnishes come in a variety of finishes including satin, gloss and flat. Choose the type of sheen you like best. Most water-based varnishes can be used inside, because they have low odor and dry quickly. Make sure you read the instructions carefully.

Crackle Medium: I think it best to use the crackle medium made to go with the brand of paint you use. Crackle mediums can be difficult to use, but if you read and follow the directions, you'll get good results. Be sure not to brush over the medium once you apply it, simply let it dry. Also, the topcoat will crack in the direction the crackle medium is brushed. To find the look you like, brush the crackle medium on a scrap of wood—thick in some areas, and thin in others. Vary the direction in which you apply the crackle—up and down, side to side and in different directions. This will help you decide on the look of the background.

Glazing Medium: This medium is used either for staining wood with the acrylic color of your choice or to mix with one of the browns like Burnt Umber to antique your painting after you're done.

Stencils: I like to use stencils for welcome signs and for backgrounds such as checks and stripes. There are thousands of stencils available for these purposes. They are easy to use and clean up with soap and water.

Gesso: Use gesso when you are wanting to seal a surface such as the back of linoleum.

Sponges: You should have a variety of sponges on hand including sea sponges, make-up sponges and regular sponges. This will help you with spills, applying paint to presses or stamps and faux finishes.

Brushes

Brushes are your most important tool when it comes to decorative painting. It is important to purchase the proper brushes for the type of work you do. You should purchase the best brushes you can afford, and take proper care of them to keep them in good shape.

The following are my brush choices. I believe that the best brush for any project is the one that works best for you. After you work with brushes, you'll discover your favorite brands, shapes and sizes. You'll want synthetic bristles for painting with acrylics.

Liner Brushes: Liners come in a variety of lengths and sizes. You'll want several sizes. I prefer the medium-length liners such as the Loew-Cornell JS liners or Robert Simmons Expressions E51. They are easier to handle than script liners and hold more paint than the short liners.

Flat Brushes: Flats are a standard in every painter's brush caddie. I don't use a lot of flat brushes in my style of painting, but you'll want several different sizes. My choice is the Loew-Cornell series 7300 shaders. I use these for foliage and basecoating.

Filbert Brushes: I use filberts most of the time rather than flat brushes, because they make great strokes with rounded ends for flowers and foliage. My choice of filbert brushes is Loew-Cornell series 7500.

Rake Brushes: I use the flat and filbert rake brushes by Loew-Cornell series 7120 and 7520. These are used for creating texture in leaves or flower petals. They can also be used for painting blades of grass.

Round Brushes: Round brushes are used for daisy petals and foliage.

All-Purpose Brush: This is a round, natural bristle brush that is available from several companies. Ceramic shops call it a ceramic dusting brush; Loew-Cornell calls it an All-Purpose Brush. It comes in several different sizes. I use one that is approximately 1-inch (2.5cm) in diameter. This is an inexpensive brush, so you may want more than one size. I use this brush to pounce in background foliage color, or to add texture to my backgrounds. It is important to use this brush dry. When you want to change colors, wipe as much of the paint as possible out of the the brush onto a paper towel.

Stencil Daubers: Stencil daubers can be used to create lettering like the Welcome Sign on page 83, or the fabulous berries on pages 92-95. Stencil daubers are usually round and come in several sizes. The size you'll need depends on the size of the berries or the size of the stencil. Stencil daubers can be found in your local craft supply store.

Miracle Wedge: The wedge is a three-sided brush with a long point. At first I was unsure what to do with it. I found it a lot of fun to use because it makes quick and easy petals and leaves.

Ultra-Round by Loew-Cornell: This round brush has a long point and holds a lot of paint. After experimenting with it, I found it makes great foliage and flower petals.

Worn Brushes: Make sure you save your old worn-out brushes, they are great for putting in background foliage. Sometimes they'll make a pretty flower or baby's breath.

Sandy's Sure Stroke: This is my favorite brush. It comes in two sizes: the original Sandy's Sure Stroke by Royal Brush or Eagle Brush's Sandy's Easy Stroke, and the Sandy's Sure Stroke Mini by Royal Brush or Eagle Brush's Sandy's Easy Stroke Mini. I saw Sandy Aubuchon use this brush to paint a carnation at the Heart of Ohio Tole Convention. I knew it would make wonderful flowers, quickly and easily. I use this brush for everything that calls for a round brush. It holds its shape well and takes the abuse of decorative painting. I recommend having both sizes handy.

Leaf Press: A press is like a rubber stamp. It can be used to quickly add leaves or even flowers. You can embellish them after you've pressed it on the surface or you can add different colors to the press itself.

Surfaces

My goal with this book is not to focus on the surfaces, but more on the techniques you'll need to do quick and easy decorative painting. Often I used to feel I couldn't paint a pattern from a book I liked, unless I had the exact surface on which the original was painted. The truth is you can paint any design on anything with a few modifications. I have painted on a canvas-covered journal I picked up in a local mall. It comes in many colors and makes a great surface for a quick painting. Every year the craft stores have a new variety of wood, glass and ceramic items. Check out the hardware stores for buckets, watering cans, mail boxes and other metal items to decorate. In my local hardware superstore I found a wonderful line of do-it-yourself furniture such as coffee tables and end tables. I also found the plain wooden ball feet that are used on a lot of sofas. They make great candleholders. You can find other items such as lamps, window shades and more at your local hardware store. A lot of stores sell glass jars of all sizes that have varnished wood lids on them. Just sand the lids a little and you're ready to basecoat and paint. Keep your eyes open and you'll be amazed at all the inexpensive, easy-to-paint-on surfaces you find.

CHAPTER CHAPTER CHAPTER CHAPTER CHAPTER CHAPTER

2

COLORS

A World of Colors

Colors make the world go round. Without them life would be very dull and boring. The following colors are the ones I use most often in my painting. I enjoy using Delta Ceramcoat acrylic paint because it is creamy, and flows well when I'm doing stroke flowers. Of course, being acrylic it cleans up quickly too. If you have a favorite brand of paint, feel free to use it. The color charts on these pages will help you match colors. Also, feel free to use other colors. Make notes of the colors that harmonize especially well, or that go with your home decor. Enjoy experimenting with colors; most of the time you'll get some surprising and beautiful results.

Color Chart: Yellows

Butter Yellow	Straw	Golden Brown
Dark Goldenrod	Antique Gold	Crocus Yellow
Calypso Orange	Poppy Orange	

Color Chart: Reds

Barn Red	Black Cherry	Mendocino
Opaque Red	Red Iron Oxide	Georgia Clay
Chocolate Cherry	Orange	Bittersweet Orange
Adobe	Nectar Coral	Rosetta Pink

Color Chart: Blues and Purples

Midnight Blue	Cadet Blue	Glacier Blue
Purple Dusk	Purple	Royal Plum
Dusty Plum	Bahama Purple	Rhythm 'n Blue
Blue Lagoon	Dusty Mauve	Copen Blue

Color Chart: Greens

Pine Green	Black Green	Seminole Green
Dark Foliage Green	Medium Foliage Green	Light Foliage Green
Boston Fern	Timberline Green	Light Timberline Green
English Yew Green	Gamal Green	

Color Chart: Browns

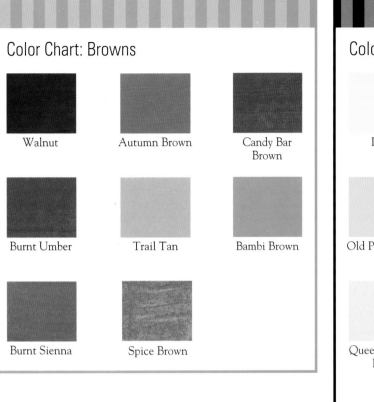

Walnut

Autumn Brown

Candy Bar Brown

Burnt Umber

Trail Tan

Bambi Brown

Burnt Sienna

Spice Brown

Color Chart: Whites

Ivory

Oyster White

Magnolia White

Old Parchment

White

Cornsilk

Queen Anne's Lace

Butter Cream

Color Chart: Darks

Black

Payne's Grey

Color Chart: Metallics

14K Gold

Silver

WHAT YOU'LL NEED TO KNOW

Terms and Techniques

Crackling

1 Basecoat your surface with either a dark color or a light color depending on what look you want. Let this dry about twenty-four hours. Once your first coat has dried, apply the crackle medium of your choice. Please follow the directions on the label.

2 When your crackle medium has dried, begin to apply the top coat. It will almost immediately begin to crackle. Don't brush over the same area twice. You'll lose your desired effect.

Sponging

1 Thin the paint with water to the consistency of ink. Use a plastic or Styrofoam plate, so your paint doesn't run.

2 Apply to the surface by tapping the sponge lightly on the surface.

3 Apply a lighter color on top of the previous sponging in the same manner, but don't cover up the original sponged color. The color used here is Light Timberline Green.

4 Add a contrasting color or a color from your design to liven up the painting and provide harmony. In this case, the color is Bittersweet Orange. As you can see, this technique provides a very subtle background.

Filbert Brush:
Comma Stroke

1 Apply pressure to the brush, pushing the bristles down and out.

2 Slowly begin to lift, turn and pull the brush toward you.

3 You should end up on the chisel edge of the brush to form the tail of the stroke. You can do this same stroke in the opposite direction as well.

Filbert Brush:
Leaf Stroke

1 Apply pressure to the brush, pushing the bristles down and out.

2 Slightly turn the brush as you lift.

3 Lift to the chisel edge to make the tip of the leaf.

Flat Brush: "S" Stroke

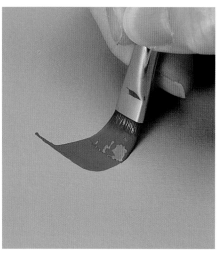

1 Touch the brush down on the chisel edge and slide toward you.

2 Begin to apply pressure, but not all the way to the ferrule.

3 Begin to release pressure as you come back to the chisel edge and slide to create the tail of the stroke.

Flat Brush: Comma Stroke

1 Using a flat brush, set it down at about a 45-degree angle.

2 Apply pressure and pull the stroke toward you.

3 As you pull the brush toward you, lift and turn the brush and slide on the chisel edge to create the tail of the stroke.

Sandy's Sure Stroke Brush: Comma Stroke

1 Touch the tip of the brush down and apply pressure.

2 Pull the brush toward you as you begin to lift the brush.

3 End on the tip of the brush to create the tail of the stroke.

Round Brush: Daisy Stroke

1 Touch the tip of the brush to your surface, but don't add pressure.

2 Pull it slightly and then add pressure creating a dip before the beginning of the comma stroke.

3 Complete the stroke as you did the comma stroke, above, and end on the tip of the brush.

Liner Brush: Comma Stroke

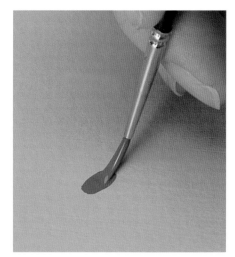 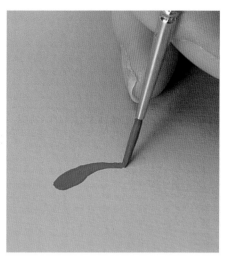 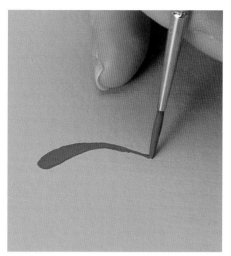

1 Touch the tip of the brush to the surface and begin to apply pressure, until you're about halfway down to the ferrule.

2 Slide the brush as you begin to lift the brush.

3 Lift to the tip of the brush and slide to create the tail.

Liner Brush: Squiggles or Vines

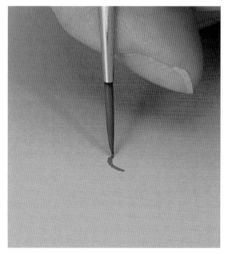 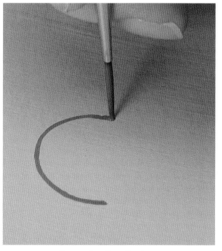 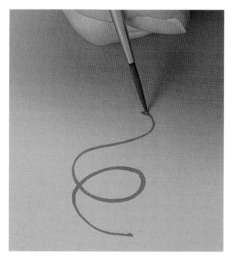

1 Thin the paint to the consistency of ink. Keep the brush on its tip.

2 Notice how the brush doesn't move. Create the squiggles by moving your whole arm, letting the bristles do the work for you.

3 Complete the stroke when you are satisfied with the squiggle by simply lifting the brush straight off the surface.

Miracle Wedge Brush: Leaf Stroke

1 For foliage and some flowers, load the brush in one color. Dip the tip of the brush in a second color.

2 Touch the tip of the brush down on the surface. Apply pressure almost to the ferrule.

3 Slide the brush toward you and slowly lift to the tip of the brush.

4 As you begin to lift the brush, notice the wonderful streaks this brush leaves behind.

5 This easy leaf stroke can be drawn out a long way to create a long thin leaf, like that of an iris or tulip.

LEAVES & TWIGS

Leaves, twigs and botanical themes are popular for today's home decor items. I love to paint them because they are so simple. With a few shades of green paint and a little imagination, you can paint leaves and botanicals to your heart's content. This is not "rocket science." This is just plain fun painting. So play with the colors and don't be afraid to experiment. You'll come up with all kinds of projects to decorate your home and to give as gifts.

Surfaces

- Mirror frame
- Coffee table

Brushes

- Sandy's Sure Stroke (approximately a no. 4 round)
- nos. 4, 6, 8, 10 filberts
- no. 1 liner
- All-Purpose brush
- Ultra-round
- no. 10 flat

Paint

- Delta Ceramcoat Acrylics

Yellow/Green Combination

Boston Fern

Light Timberline Green

Ivory

Foliage Green Combination

Dark Foliage Green

Medium Foliage Green

Light Foliage Green

Black

Ivory

Pine Green Combination

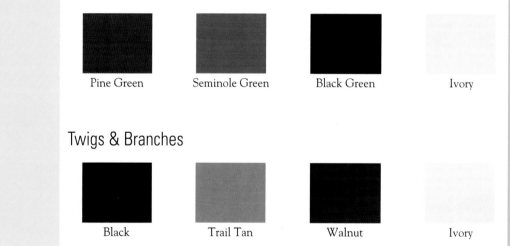

Pine Green

Seminole Green

Black Green

Ivory

Twigs & Branches

Black

Trail Tan

Walnut

Ivory

How to Double-load a Flat Brush

1 Using a no. 10 flat brush, side-load in the darker green, in this case Pine Green. You'll want to dip the corner of the brush on the edge of the paint puddle, so the brush has paint about halfway across the chisel edge and one-third of the way up the side.

2 Now, dip the other corner in the lighter color, in this case Crocus Yellow. Load this corner of the brush exactly the same as the other corner, so the colors meet in the middle.

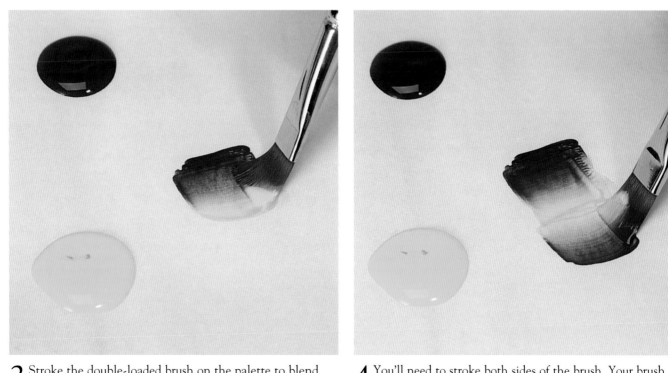

3 Stroke the double-loaded brush on the palette to blend the two colors together.

4 You'll need to stroke both sides of the brush. Your brush is now double-loaded and you're ready to paint the flat brush leaves. The double-loaded brush will allow you to shade and highlight the leaves in one stroke.

Flat Brush Leaves

Long "S" Stroke Leaves

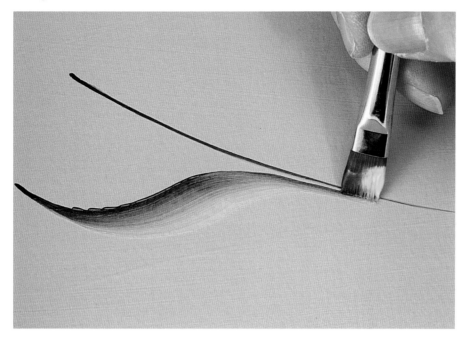

With your double-loaded brush, make an "S" stroke. Start away from the stem on the chisel edge and end on the chisel edge running into the stem. See page 20 for further instructions on making "S" strokes. Use this stroke for tulip, lily and iris leaves.

Short "S" Stroke Leaves

1 With your brush double-loaded in Pine Green and Seminole Green, make short "S" strokes to create veins in the leaves. Any darker and lighter greens will work for this technique. The darker green should face the stem. Make an "S" stroke ending with the chisel edge on the stem.

2 Create the highlight side of the leaf with a double load of Seminole Green and Light Foliage Green. Again the darker color faces the stem. Turn your work to make painting as comfortable as possible.

3 The strokes get smaller as you get closer to the leaf tip. Fill in the entire leaf with these strokes.

The Completed Leaf

Filbert Brush Leaves

Single-Stroke Leaves

1 Double-load the filbert brush with Pine Green and Seminole Green. Any size brush will work and any two greens. Begin on the chisel edge.

2 Apply pressure to the bristles and slide the brush toward you.

3 Lift up onto the chisel edge and slide to create the tip.

4 Connect the leaves to the stem using a liner brush loaded with Pine Green or the darker green you used in the double load.

The Completed Leaf Spray

Filbert Brush Leaves, continued

Two-Stroke Leaves

1 Using a no. 10 filbert brush double-loaded with Pine Green and Seminole Green, pull in the stem. Use the chisel edge of the brush to do so.

2 Start on the chisel edge, just as you did for the single-stroke filbert leaves. Apply pressure to make the fat part of the leaf, then lift up to the chisel edge.

3 For the second stroke, do not flip the brush. Make the same stroke about halfway on the first stroke. Apply pressure to the brush.

4 Slide back up to the chisel edge and into the tip of the first stroke.

5 Using the liner brush loaded with Pine Green, pull from the stem into the leaf following the dark and light line in between the two strokes.

Round Brush Comma Stroke Leaves

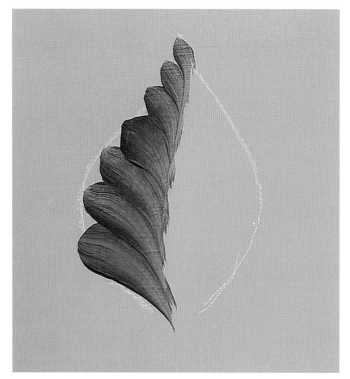

1 Begin at the base of the leaf, using the Sandy's Sure Stroke round brush double-loaded with Pine Green and Seminole Green. With Seminole Green facing the tip of the leaf, make comma strokes with the tail ending in the center vein. For more information on comma strokes see page 21.

2 To create the highlight side of the leaf, double-load the Sandy's Sure Stroke with Light Foliage Green and Seminole Green. Again, make your comma strokes go into the center vein. Turn your work to make painting more comfortable.

3 As you get closer to the tip of the leaf, the comma strokes get smaller, but all pull into the center vein.

The Completed Comma Stroke Leaf

Ultra-Round Long Thin Leaves

1 Load one side of an Ultra-round brush with Pine Green and the other with Light Foliage Green. Start the stroke on the tip of the brush.

2 Apply pressure so the bristles spread out to the width of the leaf and slide.

3 Slowly come back to the tip of the brush as you pull into the stem.

Cluster of Long Thin Leaves

Background Foliage

1 Using the All-Purpose brush, load in the darkest green, in this case Black Green. Pat the brush on the palette to remove excess paint. Pounce in the area you want background foliage. Do not clean the brush.

2 Without cleaning the brush, load with the medium green, in this case Seminole Green. Pat again on the palette to remove some paint. Without covering the previous background, pounce Seminole Green toward the middle of the same area. Do not wash the brush.

3 Pick up Ivory on one side of the brush and Light Foliage Green on the other. Blend by patting these colors together on the palette. Pounce lightly over the same area, but without covering the previous colors. Keep this area light and airy-looking.

Twigs and Branches

1 Load a no. 1 liner brush with Black on one side and Walnut on the other. Press down on the bristles and wiggle the brush a little as you pull it toward you.

2 As you pull the stroke toward you, begin to lift the brush back to the tip of the bristles.

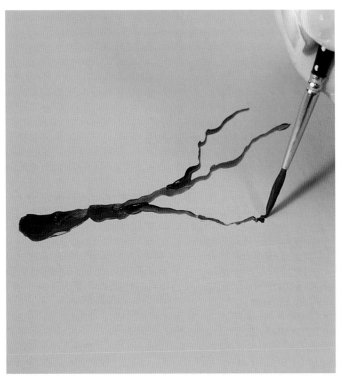

3 Pull side twigs off the main branch using the same technique. Start on the main branch and pull the brush, wiggling the brush as you pull it toward you.

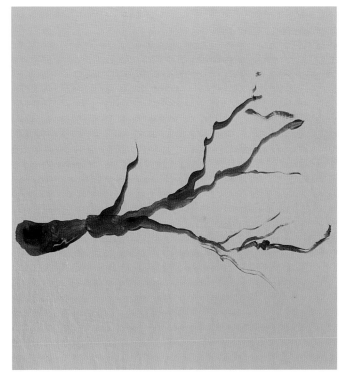

The Completed Branch

More Leaf Ideas...

Have fun and use your imagination. Mix and match these leaves with the fruit and flowers in this book. You'll have endless possibilities for your painting pleasure. Here are a few more ideas to get you started.

Small one-stroke and two-stroke leaves are combined with oranges to make wonderful art for the kitchen.

Long thin "S" stroke leaves are combined with tulips to make a beautiful wall plaque.

A simple mirror frame is turned into a striking ornament for fall.

Background foliage and tiny one-stroke leaves are an easy decoration for this clock.

With parts from your local home center, you can make this lovely coffee table to decorate your home.

FILLER FLOWERS

F iller flowers are wonderful additions to almost any project, or if you're looking for a quick gift, these flowers can be applied to any surface. Mix and match these little lovelies with each other, larger flowers, fruit or all of them for a spectacular work of art. Take a look at the idea section (pages 54-55) to spark your creativity and provide you with endless possibilities for these quick and easy flowers that fit in anywhere.

Patterns

Daisies & tiny five-petal flowers

Coreopsis

Mini-Roses

These patterns may be hand-traced or photocopied for personal use only. They are shown here full size.

Sweet Williams

These patterns may be hand-traced or photocopied for personal use only. They are shown here full size.

Lilacs

One O'clocks

Coreopsis

1 Double-load a no. 8 flat with Black Cherry and Butter Yellow. Don't overblend. Begin the stroke with the Black Cherry toward the center. Wiggle the brush back and forth to create the petal.

2 Wiggle the brush to the other side of the petal and end on the chisel edge.

3 Be sure you turn the brush as you wiggle to follow the petal shapes.

4 Pat the coreopsis center with a small flat brush loaded with Burnt Sienna.

5 Using a no. 1 liner loaded with Butter Yellow, add dots around the center. Wash the brush.

6 Using the same brush loaded with Magnolia White, add a few more dots for variety.

7 Using the liner brush, pat a little Black in the center.

8 Add little two-stroke leaves using Light Foliage Green and Black Green double-loaded on a no. 6 filbert.

Sweet William

1 Double-load a no. 8 flat brush with Purple and White. Do not blend too much. You want to keep the white edge strong. Start on the chisel edge.

2 Press down and wiggle, slightly turning the brush. Come back to the chisel edge. Slightly overlap the petals.

3 With the petals completed, it's time to work on the center.

4 Pat a little White in the center of the Sweet William petals using the no. 8 flat. Wash the brush.

5 Pat a bit of Seminole Green around the outer edge of the wet White center. This will keep the white from being so stark.

6 Add dots of Seminole Green using the no. 1 liner brush around the edge of the center.

7 To complete the Sweet William, add the one-stroke leaves with a no. 6 flat brush double-loaded with Light Foliage Green and White.

Fuchsia

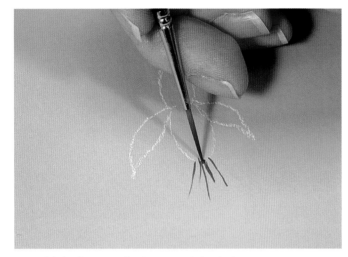

1 Add the lines at the bottom of the fuchsia, using a no. 1 liner loaded with Black Cherry.

2 Fill in the bottom of the fuchsia using a no. 6 filbert brush loaded with Purple.

3 Fill in the calyx with Black Cherry using a no. 6 filbert brush.

4 Paint the outside petals with Black Cherry using the same filbert brush as you did for the calyx.

5 Paint the two-stroke leaves with a no. 6 flat brush double-loaded with Pine Green and Seminole Green. Add the stem using a no. 1 liner brush loaded with Purple.

Aster

1 Load a no. 1 liner brush with Copen Blue. Make long comma strokes from the outer edge of the aster to the center. The tail isn't important because it will be covered up.

2 Load the no. 1 liner brush with a brush mix of Copen Blue and Magnolia White. Repeat the comma strokes, but make them a little shorter.

3 Load the no. 1 liner brush with Magnolia White. Make your comma strokes a little shorter.

4 Pat in the center using the Sandy's Sure Stroke round brush loaded with Golden Brown. Don't wash the brush.

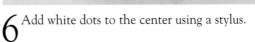

5 Shade the outer edge of the center with Candy Bar Brown using the dirty brush. Pat as you did in the last step.

6 Add white dots to the center using a stylus.

Mini-Roses

1 Double-load a ³⁄₈-inch (10mm) angular brush with Payne's Grey and Magnolia White. Stroke an upside down "U".

2 Finish the bowl of the rose with a right-side-up "U" stroke. Make sure the center is rounded with the lightest top edge and bottom edge connecting.

3 Using the same brush double-loaded with the Payne's Grey and Magnolia White, paint the right petal with a comma stroke.

4 Paint the left petal using the same double load and the same stroke in the opposite direction.

5 Paint the right flip stroke petal, like the comma stroke, but smaller.

6 Paint the left flip stroke petal in the same manner.

7 Slide the brush from one side of the center to the other to create the middle petal. The dark side of the brush is toward the center.

8 Add the mini-dashes near the bowl to complete the mini-rose.

Rosebud

1 Double-load the ⅜-inch (10mm) angular brush with Payne's Grey and White. Make the upside-down "U".

2 Using the same brush make the "U" stroke to complete the bud. Make sure the center is round.

3 Paint the calyx using a no. 4 filbert brush double-loaded with Pine Green and Seminole Green. Add pressure to the brush, turn and lift up to the chisel edge.

4 Add the second calyx petal and the stem in the same way. Turn your work to make painting more comfortable.

Lilacs

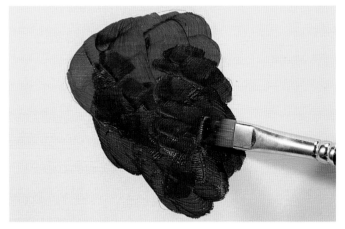

1 Using a no. 10 flat brush, basecoat the lilac area with Midnight Blue and Purple. Place colors randomly to fill in the area and mix the colors on the surface where they meet.

2 With little push strokes, using the no. 4 filbert brush, create the flower petals in the background. Use Purple and Bahama Purple in the lighter areas and Midnight Blue and Blue Lagoon in the darker areas.

3 For the lighter petal colors, use a mix of the previous colors plus Magnolia White. Add these petals using the dirty brush from the previous steps.

4 Add the lilac centers using a stylus dipped in Straw.

5 Paint the lilac leaves using the no. 6 filbert brush double-loaded with Pine Green and Medium Foliage Green.

6 For the highlight side of the leaf, double-load the same brush with Medium Foliage Green and Light Foliage Green. Make the "S" strokes into the center.

One O'clocks

1 Paint the tiny one-stroke leaves around the area of flowers using a no. 4 filbert brush loaded with Pine Green.

2 Paint the flowers with Purple, Bahama Purple and Glacier Blue, using the Sandy's Sure Stroke brush. Touch down lightly on just the brush tip to make a dab of paint.

3 Dab in the centers with Candy Bar Brown using Sandy's Sure Stroke Brush.

4 Paint dot flower petals on the outside of the cluster using a stylus dipped in Antique Gold.

5 Dot the flower centers with a stylus dipped in Candy Bar Brown.

Johnny Jump-ups

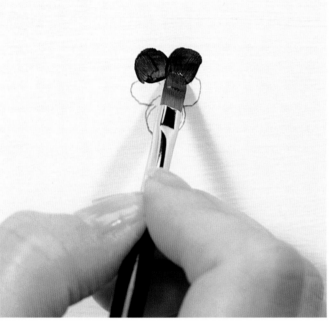

1 Load a no. 4 filbert brush with a brush mix of Royal Plum and Crocus Yellow. Touch the brush down and pull toward the center.

2 Pick up a little Crocus Yellow on the tip of the brush and pull in the side petals.

3 Pick up more Crocus Yellow on the brush and add the center petal in the same manner as you did the others.

4 Add the Crocus Yellow center using a no. 1 liner. The Black lines are added with the same brush.

Forget-me-nots

1 Pat in the background using the All-Purpose brush with a grouping of the greens listed on page 26.

2 Make a cluster of these tiny blossoms made up of "C" strokes using the no. 4 flat brush double-loaded with Midnight Blue and Magnolia White.

3 Add the two-stroke leaves using a no. 4 filbert brush double-loaded with Pine Green and Seminole Green.

4 Add a dot for the center using a stylus dipped in Antique Gold.

More Filler Flower Ideas...

This wonderful sampler board of filler flowers can be used as a trivet for your table, as coasters, or as a wall decoration for your kitchen.

Add similar flowers to wooden jar lids and cooking utensils in colors picked up from your kitchen decor.

Cute trinket boxes make wonderful gifts for friends, kids, just about anyone.

A few filler flowers on the base of a hurricane lamp or on a jar lid can be changed to represent the seasons or holidays.

Mini-roses look great on almost any surface. Dress them up with ribbon and you've got a great gift for friends or family.

FOCAL FLOWERS

F ocal flowers are the large flowers that are at the focal point, or center of interest, of each of my designs. The flowers are generally easy to paint, just like the filler flowers and leaves. The nice thing about these flowers is you can paint them almost any color. Paint them to match your decor, or fill in the design with complementing filler flowers and leaves, and voilá, you've created your own unique design.

A Basket of Spring

Materials

Surface
- Blank Journal

Brushes
- no. 10 filbert
- 1/2-inch angular shader
- no. 1 liner

Delta Ceramcoat Paint

- Butter Yellow
- Burnt Sienna
- Poppy Orange
- White
- Light Foliage Green
- Dark Foliage Green
- Spice Brown
- Black
- Burnt Umber
- Ivory
- Bambi Brown
- Pine Green

On a trip to the mall, I came across some blank journals in a variety of colors. I knew they would look great with large flowers or fruit designs. When you paint this type of project with several different flowers, paint the background foliage, then paint the largest flowers and finish with the filler flowers and leaves until you're satisfied.

1 Basecoat the basket with Bambi Brown. Pounce some background with the All-Purpose brush with Dark Foliage Green and Pine Green.

2 Add dark shading under the rim and down the left side of the basket with Burnt Umber. Double load a no. 8 flat brush with Bambi Brown and Burnt Umber. Make S strokes on the handle and rim.

3 Use the no. 1 liner brush loaded with Spice Brown and then Burnt Umber to paint the scribble lines on the basket. Add a few more lines with Black. Then add the light lines on the right with Ivory.

Paint the Daffodils

1 Basecoat the daffodil petals with a no. 10 filbert brush loaded with Butter Yellow. You may need two coats.

2 Using a ½-inch (12mm) angular shader sideloaded with Burnt Sienna, add the shading on the trumpet.

3 Pat a little Poppy Orange down the throat of the daffodil using a ½-inch (12mm) angular shader.

4 Using a no. 1 liner brush loaded with White, dab around the edge of the bowl.

5 Overstroke the daffodil petals with a no. 10 filbert double-loaded with Butter Yellow and White.

6 Paint two strokes. Make sure the white side of the brush is facing the left for both strokes.

7 Using a liner brush loaded with thinned Burnt Sienna, pull lines from the bowl's base toward the top.

The Completed Daffodil

Using Sandy's Sure Stroke brush double-loaded with Light Foliage Green and Pine Green, pull in the stems and paint the bumpy leaves. Add a few Black dots in the throat using the no. 1 liner brush. For instructions on how to paint the basket turn to page 58. For instructions on how to paint the foliage turn to page 36. For instructions on how to paint the daisies turn to page 115.

Basket of Spring

This pattern may be hand-traced or photocopied for personal use only. Enlarge at 109% to bring up to full size.

Tulips in a Basket

Materials

Surface
- ¾-inch board cut to desired shape

Brushes
- Sandy's Sure Stroke
- Sandy's Sure Stroke Mini
- nos. 4, 6, 8 & 10 filberts
- 18/0 liner
- All-Purpose brush
- ½-inch angular shader
- no. 10 flat

Delta Ceramcoat Paint
- Midnight Blue
- Old Parchment
- Black
- Autumn Brown
- Trail Tan
- Burnt Umber
- Royal Plum
- Queen Anne's Lace
- Magnolia White
- Antique Gold
- Candy Bar Brown
- Ivory
- Pine Green
- Seminole Green
- Dusty Mauve

Supplies
- Delta Crackle Medium

My dad cut this board for me. It is 7¼ x 19 inches. He cut a rounded top on the board and I placed the basket and the three tulips, leaves and filler flowers in the basket until it suited me.

Prepare the Surface

Basecoat the board with two coats of Midnight Blue, using a large flat brush. When the basecoat is completely dry, apply a coat of Delta Crackle Medium, following the directions. When the crackle medium is dry apply a top coat of Old Parchment. Do not go over your strokes again or the paint will smear over the crackle medium. Once this has dried you can apply a basic pattern, if you want to.

Paint the Tulips

1 Double-load a no. 10 flat brush with Royal Plum and Queen Anne's Lace. Stroke the brush back and forth on your palette to achieve a nice blend. Paint the side petals of the tulips with S strokes.

2 Using Sandy's Sure Stroke brush, load Royal Plum fully on the brush and pull through Queen Anne's Lace on one side of the brush. Face the light color to the ceiling, make a push stroke, pulling the tail of the stroke toward the stem.

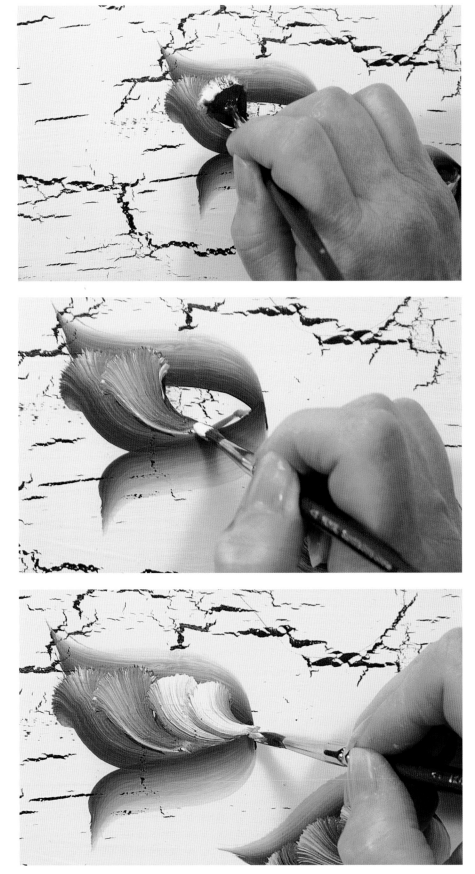

3 To create the middle strokes, place the Sure Stroke brush down and push the bristles, so they open. Be careful not to push down to the ferrule. Push the brush away from you into the stroke.

4 Once you've pushed the brush into the stroke, finish the stroke by pulling toward you and into the stem to create the tail of the stroke.

5 Finish the center petals of the tulip using the push-pull stroke. Make the strokes smaller as you get close to the stem. Paint the other two tulips in the design the same way.

Paint the Stems, Leaves & Basket

1 Basecoat the basket with Burnt Umber, using a large flat brush. Double-load a flattened Sandy's Sure Stroke brush with Pine Green on one side and Seminole Green on the other. Pull the stems from the tulip into the basket.

2 Using the no. 10 flat brush, double-loaded with Pine Green and Seminole Green, paint long "S" strokes for the leaves. Turn the piece so it is comfortable for you to pull the stroke from the basket out toward the tulip.

3 The tulips and stems are now complete. It's time to work on the basket.

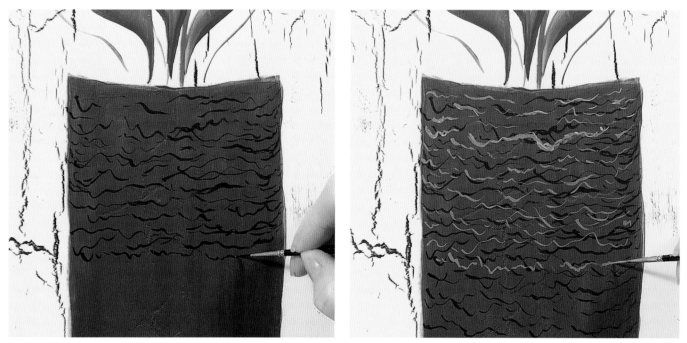

4 Using a no. 1 liner brush loaded with Black, make wiggly lines from one side of the basket to the other. These are random lines and do not need to be precise.

5 Using the same liner brush loaded with Autumn Brown, make more wiggly lines like the ones you did previously. Do not completely cover the basket.

6 Make wiggly lines using the liner brush loaded with Trail Tan.

7 Add wiggly highlights to the basket using the liner brush loaded with Ivory.

8 Complete the basket by using a no. 10 flat brush, double-loaded with Burnt Umber and Autumn Brown, to make a series of "S" strokes across the rim of the basket to form the edge.

Paint the Pink Flowers and Leaves

1 Using a filbert brush loaded with Dusty Mauve, begin placing the filler flowers in randomly. The filler flowers in this lesson are the same as the lilacs on page 50.

2 Using a filbert brush, place small filler leaves and stems. Use a comma stroke with a variety of greens. Do not clean your brush in-between colors.

3 Using your filbert brush loaded with Dusty Mauve plus a little bit of Magnolia White on one side of the brush, make some five petal flowers randomly placed.

4 Using the same dirty brush, make the lightest flowers by adding more white and paint a few of the lightest five petal flowers.

5 Using your liner brush, add Antique Gold dots to form the center of the five petal flowers. Next, add Candy Bar Brown dots to the center.

6 Using Sandy's Sure Stroke Mini brush, place filler flowers and stems. The flower petals are touch and lift strokes using Old Parchment. Paint the stems Pine Green.

7 Using the Sure Stroke Mini brush, add a few more flowers with white. If you use two different colors when you do these small flowers, they will be more interesting.

8 Add the flower centers with a no. 1 liner brush double loaded with Antique Gold and Candy Bar Brown.

Tulips in a Basket

This pattern may be hand-traced or
photocopied for personal use only.
Enlarge at 125% to bring up to full size.

A Sign of Carnations

The carnation, a lovely little summer flower, is used often in arrangements. This house address sign will make sure your home looks like summer all year long.

Materials

Surface
- Wooden Sign Board (available at craft stores)

Brushes
- Sandy's Sure Stroke
- no. 6 filbert

Delta Ceramcoat Paint
- Black Cherry
- Barn Red
- Oyster White
- Medium Foliage Green
- Dark Foliage Green

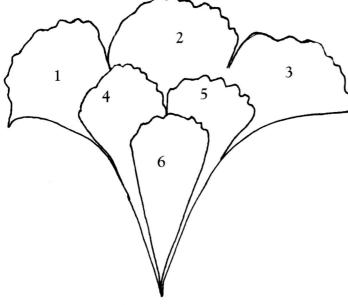

How to Paint the Petals

Follow this diagram to help you paint the carnation petals. After you have completed the carnation, paint the "bumpy" leaves using a no. 6 filbert brush double loaded with Dark Foliage Green and Medium Foliage Green. Use a push down, release, push down, release stroke and pull to the stem.

This pattern may be hand-traced or photocopied for personal use only. Enlarge at 200% to bring up to full size.

Paint the Carnation

1 Load the Sure Stroke brush with Black Cherry and Barn Red. Press the brush almost to the ferrule and fan out the bristles.

2 Push the brush forward to create the feathery edge.

3 Pull the brush back to the tip and toward the stem. Paint about five petals on the back row.

4 Load the brush with Barn Red and Oyster White. Repeat the push-pull stroke for the mid-layer of about three petals.

5 Add more Oyster White to the brush and create the top layer of of about one petal using the push-pull stroke as before.

6 Add the leaves and stems with Medium and Dark Foliage Green double-loaded on Sandy's Sure Stroke brush.

Lilies

Materials

Surface
- Oval Plaque (available at craft stores)

Brushes
- Miracle Wedge brush
- no. 1 liner

Delta Ceramcoat Paint
- Light Foliage Green
- Pine Green
- Dark Goldenrod
- Straw
- Magnolia White
- Georgia Clay

1 Apply the leaves using a Miracle Wedge brush loaded with Light Foliage Green and tipped in Pine Green. Make a long leaf stroke, starting from the outside and pulling to the stem.

Paint the Lily

1 Triple load a Miracle Wedge brush with Dark Goldenrod, Straw and Magnolia White. Press the bristles down almost to the ferrule to spread them out half the width of the petal.

2 Paint each petal with two or three leaf strokes, starting with the ones underneath and pulling them into the flower center. The next layer of petals goes over the first. All of the flower petals are painted in the same manner.

3 Slowly release the pressure on the brush as you come to the center. Return to the point of the brush as you complete each stroke.

4 Gently wipe the brush on a damp paper towel removing some of the paint. Reload by tipping in Magnolia White.

Paint the Lily, continued

5 As you complete the petals that are behind, wipe the brush and reload, tipping in Magnolia White.

6 Turn your work as needed to make painting more comfortable. Begin layering the petals on top.

7 Apply a third stroke to the petal if needed to fill in the petal. Wipe the paint out of the brush. Start from the outside edge and pull this stroke down the center over the two previous strokes.

8 Paint the center of the lily with a no. 1 liner brush loaded with Light Foliage Green. Pull a curved line stroke from the center out. Clean your brush.

9 Using the no. 1 liner brush, add dots of Georgia Clay to the center. Touch the tip of the brush in Straw and add dots to the end of the stamens.

10 Load the liner brush in Georgia Clay and add tiny dots to the petals.

11 Add a saying with a stamp or create your own lettering. If you're using a stamp, remember to lift straight up, so you don't smear the saying.

Lilies

This pattern may be hand-traced or
photocopied for personal use only.
It is shown here full size.

Poinsettia & Holly

Holiday decorations are a snap when you use this method of creating poinsettias and holly berries. Combine them with fruit and other flowers and you'll have a treat to delight your holiday guests.

Materials

Surface
- Piece of scrap linoleum approx. $2\frac{1}{2}$ x 3 feet

Brushes
- no. 6 flat
- no. 1 liner
- Ultra-round
- stencil dauber

Delta Ceramcoat Paint
- Black Green
- Pine Green
- Light Foliage Green
- Barn Red
- Magnolia White
- Seminole Green
- Butter Yellow
- Dusty Mauve
- Black Cherry
- Chocolate Cherry

Holly Leaves & Berries

1 Double load a no. 6 flat brush with Black Green and Pine Green. With the darkest color to the outside edge, follow the leaf contour, painting half of the leaf. Load the brush with Pine Green and Light Foliage Green. With the light color to the outside edge, paint the other half. Add the stem and vein with Black Green loaded on a no. 1 liner brush.

2 Paint the berries by tapping one side of the stencil dauber in Barn Red and the other in Magnolia White. Pat the dauber on your palette to slightly blend the colors. Put the dauber in place and add pressure to create a berry.

3 Lift straight up. Paint about three berries per leaf. Reload the stencil dauber if needed.

Poinsettia

1 Using an Ultra-round brush loaded with Barn Red, pull two strokes from the outside tip into the center to complete each petal just like the two-stroke leaves. Paint all the lower petals in the same manner. (See page 32 for further instruction on two-stroke leaves.)

2 With the same dirty brush wiped on a paper towel, pick up Dusty Mauve. Paint the same two-strokes, but make this layer in-between the first layer of petals. Then, in-between the second layer of petals, paint slightly shorter strokes with the dirty brush plus Magnolia White.

3 With a no. 1 liner brush loaded with Black Cherry, paint the veins on the petals. You can use Chocolate Cherry if you want darker veins.

4 Completed veins.

5 Pat in the center with a no. 1 liner brush loaded with Seminole Green.

6 Add dots of Butter Yellow to the green center, using your stylus or liner brush.

7 Add smaller dots of Barn Red on top of the yellow dots using the stylus or liner brush.

8 Completed poinsettia.

Poinsettia & Holly

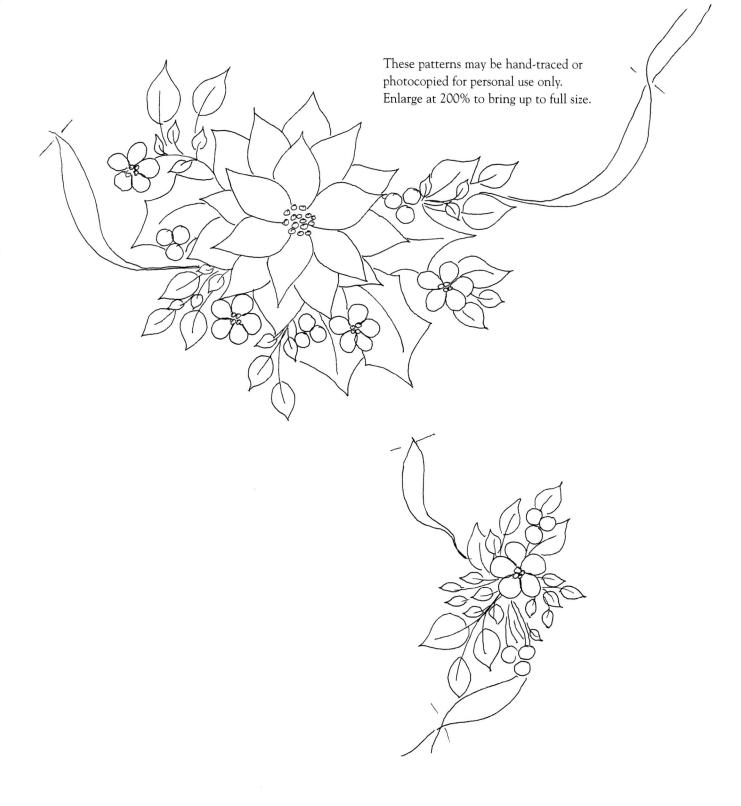

These patterns may be hand-traced or
photocopied for personal use only.
Enlarge at 200% to bring up to full size.

Zinnia

Materials

Surface
- Small metal bucket (available at craft and hardware stores)

Brushes
- no. 8 filbert
- no. 1 liner

Delta Ceramcoat Paint
- Rhythm 'n Blue
- Bahama Purple
- Boston Fern
- Black
- Black Green
- White

The zinnia is another very easy flower to design with and paint. You need three values of one color, but you can use blue, purple, orange, yellow or red so your design is in harmony and balanced.

It's fun to use this project as a candle holder on a patio. Simply put sand in the bottom of the container, insert your candle and you're ready for entertaining.

1 Paint two-stroke leaves around where the blossom will be. Load a no. 8 filbert brush with Rhythm 'n Blue. Paint the edge petals with flat strokes.

2 With the dirty brush, add the next layer of petals with Bahama Purple. These strokes are longer on one side to create a slightly "off-center" center.

Zinnia

This pattern may be hand-traced or photocopied for personal use only. Enlarge at 189% to bring up to full size.

3 To your dirty brush, add a little white and paint the next layer of petals. Continue to add white to the brush until you reach the very center of the flower.

4 Pat in the center with Boston Fern loaded on a no. 1 liner brush.

5 Add dots of Black around the outer edge of the green center using the no. 1 liner brush.

6 With Black Green on the liner brush, add the stems and curlicues to complete the Zinnia.

A Mum Welcome

Welcome everyone to your house with your very own Mum welcome sign. It's easy and fun. Best of all, when you're done you'll have another set of flowers that you can incorporate into your own designs.

Basecoat the board with Black Green mixed with Glazing Medium (1:1). Test your color on the back of your surface. It should look like a dark green stain. Paint the edge of the board with Antique Gold and

let dry. Mix Burnt Sienna and Glazing Medium (1:1). Brush this over the Antique Gold to give an antique look.

Materials

Surface
- Half-round wooden board

Brushes
- Sandy's Sure Stroke
- no. 4 filbert
- nos. 1 & 2 liner
- scruffy brush

Delta Ceramcoat Paint
- Pine Green
- Seminole Green
- Magnolia White
- Adobe Red
- Nectar Coral
- Rosetta Pink
- Queen Anne's Lace
- Antique Gold
- Candy Bar Brown
- Black
- Bambi Brown
- Autumn Brown

1 Double load Sandy's Sure Stroke brush with Pine Green and Seminole Green. With the Pine Green side facing the base of the leaf, pull comma strokes from the outer edge of the leaf toward the center using the tail of the comma to help form the veins. The comma strokes get shorter as you get closer to the leaf tip.

2 Double load your Sandy's Sure Stroke with Seminole Green and Magnolia White. With the Seminole Green side of the brush facing the base of the leaf, pull comma strokes as you did in the previous step.

3 Using the tip of your round brush, pat Candy Bar Brown into the center area (bowl) of the mum.

4 While the Candy Bar Brown is still wet, pat Black in at the lower edge of the bowl. Blend the colors to shade.

5 Using Sandy's Sure Stroke brush and Adobe Red, pull in the back petals. Start in the center and use bumpy strokes to create the ruffled back edge. Then, go back to the center and paint the strokes on the opposite side of the flower.

6 With the Sure Stroke brush loaded with Adobe Red, pull in comma strokes. Pull each of the strokes toward the stem.

 creative hint:

    When you paint any flower, visualize the point where the stem would attach and pull your strokes toward that point. If it helps, you can make a dot at that point and use it as a target to pull your strokes toward.

7 With the Sure Stroke brush loaded with Adobe Red, pull the comma strokes to form the skirt. The side strokes are curved more. Pull all strokes toward the stem.

8 With the Sure Stroke brush loaded with Adobe Red, pull the strokes in the center of the skirt straighter, but still end toward the stem.

9 Load the "dirty" brush with Nectar Coral and pull in a lighter layer of comma strokes on the ball of the mum.

10 Stroke a lighter layer of petals on the skirt using the same "dirty" brush loaded with Nectar Coral. Each layer of strokes will be a little shorter and lighter.

11 Use the "dirty" brush loaded with Rosetta Pink and Queen Anne's Lace to add a few lighter strokes to the ball of the flower.

12 Add a few comma strokes to the skirt using the colors from the previous step.

13 With a no. 1 liner brush, add a few dots to the center of the flower using Antique Gold, White and Black.

Paint the Aster

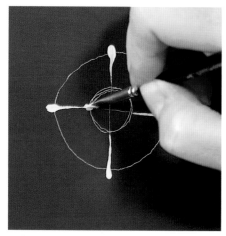

1 Load a no. 4 filbert with Magnolia White. Form the first four petals with the "drop-pull stroke."

2 Apply pressure to the side of the brush to form a tear drop shape. Release the pressure, pulling a thin line toward the center.

3 Continue by placing strokes in the center of each section, until each area is complete.

4 The second layer of strokes is shorter than the first. Place these strokes in-between the first layer of strokes.

5 Use only a few strokes for the third layer to fill in any gaps.

This pattern may be hand-traced or photocopied for personal use only. It is shown here full size.

6 Pat Antique Gold in the center using Sandy's Sure Stroke. Let this dry before continuing.

7 Double-load a scruffy brush with Candy Bar Brown and Antique Gold. With Candy Bar Brown toward the outside edge, pat blend the colors.

8 Add dots to the center edge with the tip of the liner brush loaded with Black.

9 Add a few white dots using the liner brush.

Add Filler Flowers

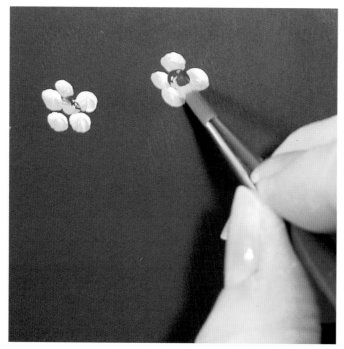

1 Load your Sandy's Sure Stroke with Antique Gold and pull through Magnolia White on one side. With the White facing the right, touch the brush tip to the surface and push slightly toward "one o'clock." Repeat for each petal, usually five petals per flower. Load the brush with Antique Gold and Candy Bar Brown. With the Brown facing the right, slightly push the brush tip toward "one o'clock" to form the center.

2 Pull in the small comma strokes to form the ball of the spoon mum bud using a no. 2 liner loaded with Magnolia White. Be sure to follow the shape of the flower and pull toward the stem. Pull the skirt strokes using the no. 2 liner loaded with Magnolia White. Make sure to follow the shape of the flower and pull toward the stem.

3 To make the spoon mum buds, use the no. 4 filbert brush and the "drop-pull stroke." Pull a few random strokes toward the stem.

4 Use the filbert brush double-loaded with Pine Green and Seminole Green to pull two "S" strokes to form the calyx. Pull in the stem using the no. 1 liner brush.

5 Pull comma strokes to form the ball of the flower using the Sandy's Sure Stroke brush loaded with Adobe Red. Use less pressure to form small strokes.

6 Pull strokes to form the skirt using Sandy's Sure Stroke loaded with Adobe Red. Use the dirty brush loaded with Rosetta Pink to pull the highlight strokes to the ball skirt of the flower.

7 Use a stencil for the lettering, or if you feel brave you can freehand it. Apply the base color, Bambi Brown, with a stencil brush. Then add a little Autumn Brown with the stencil brush. This gives the lettering a little texture and a softer appearance.

FRUITS & BERRIES

Fruit is one of my favorite subjects to paint. It is diverse enough that it can be painted separately or with some of the flowers in this book.

When I think of fruit, I think about my grandmother's kitchen and the ripe fruits ready to be canned. I don't have time or the patience to can fruit, but I do have time to paint my kitchen decor to imitate these luscious goodies. I hope you enjoy these quick and easy projects with surfaces you can find just about anywhere.

Blueberries

1 Basecoat the blueberries using a no. 6 filbert brush loaded with Cadet Blue.

2 With a ½-inch (12mm) angular brush corner-loaded with Midnight Blue, shade one edge of the berries.

3 Dab little dots of Oyster White with your no. 1 liner brush on the edge opposite the shading.

4 Add a few one-stroke leaves with Light, Medium and Dark Foliage Greens loaded on a no. 6 filbert brush. Add a blossom end using Black. Paint the stems and curlicues using a no. 1 liner brush to complete the blueberries.

Cherries

1 Basecoat the cherries using a stencil dauber and Mendocino Red as your base color. Pick up Black Cherry on one side and pounce on the cherries to shade. Highlight with Magnolia White.

2 Using a no. 4 filbert brush, add the stems, leaves and curlicues using a variety of the Light, Medium and Dark Foliage colors. The yellow dots are added for interest using a stylus and Crocus Yellow.

Strawberries

Blackberries & Raspberries

These patterns may be hand-traced or photocopied for personal use only. They are shown here full size.

Strawberries

1 Basecoat the strawberry with Barn Red using a no. 10 filbert brush.

2 Float Chocolate Cherry using a ½-inch (12mm) angular brush on the left side of the berry for shading. Float Orange on the right half of the berry using a ½-inch (12mm) angle brush to create the highlight.

3 Paint the sepals with a no. 4 filbert brush double-loaded with Seminole Green and Pine Green.

4 Paint the seeds using no. 1 liner brush loaded with Black.

5 Highlight the seeds with Butter Yellow on the right half of the seed using a no. 1 liner brush.

Blackberries & Raspberries

1 Basecoat half the raspberry with Black Cherry and half with Dusty Mauve using a no. 4 filbert brush. Pat the colors together in the middle to create a gradation of values.

2 With a hard-packed Q-tip, pick up White. Pat some of the color off on your palette. Stamp down around the berry to make the seed pockets. This step must be done in wet paint.

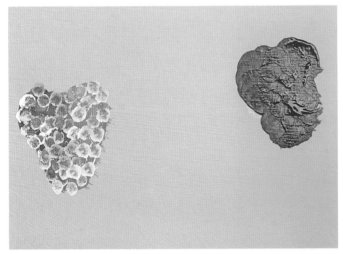

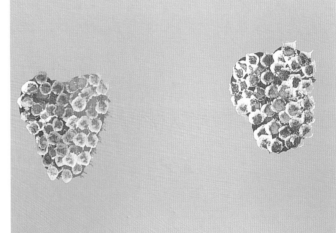

3 Basecoat the blackberries with Midnight Blue on the left and Purple on the right with a no. 4 filbert brush.

4 While the paint is still wet, pat a hard-packed Q-tip in White as you did for the raspberry. Make the seed pockets with the loaded Q-tip. Don't make too many pockets.

5 Paint the one-stroke leaves with a no. 6 filbert brush double-loaded with Black Green and Seminole Green. Use a no. 1 liner brush to paint the stems.

Pear

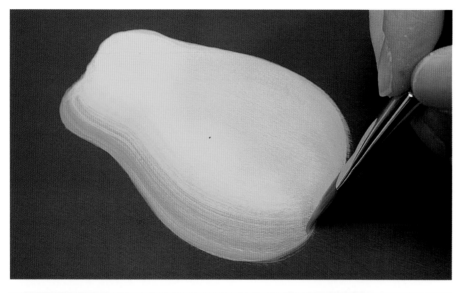

1 Basecoat the pear with Butter Yellow. Using a ½-inch (12mm) angular shader double-loaded with Orange and Butter Yellow, float orange on the left half of the pear to create a shadow.

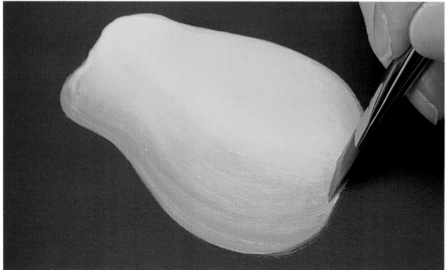

2 Walk the orange toward the center of the pear using the double-loaded ½-inch (12mm) angular shader.

Pear

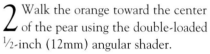

This pattern may be hand-traced or photocopied for personal use only. Enlarge at 125% to bring it up to full size.

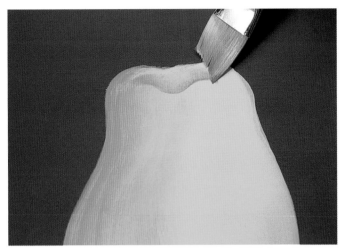

3 Corner-load the ½-inch (12mm) angular shader with Burnt Sienna. Paint the indent at the top of the pear.

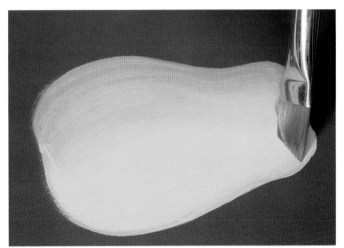

4 Float Light Foliage Green on the right half of the pear using the ½-inch (12mm) angular shader. Walk the color toward the center of the pear.

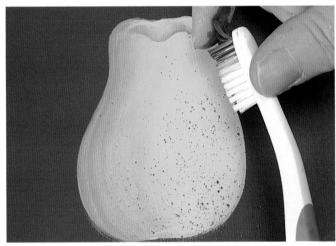

5 Using an old toothbrush loaded with thinned Black Cherry, flyspeck the pear, especially the right half.

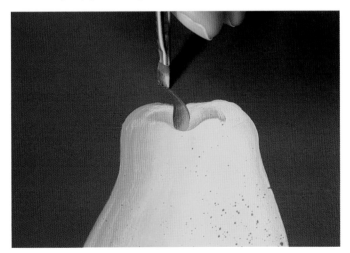

6 Paint the pear stem with a no. 4 flat brush double-loaded with Bambi Brown and Candy Bar Brown.

7 Paint the leaves with a no. 10 flat brush double-loaded with Boston Fern and Timberline Green. Using the no. 1 liner brush loaded with Timberline Green, paint the veins and curlicues.

Apple

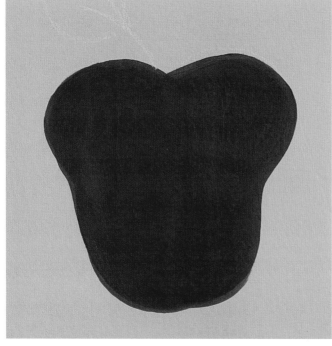

1 Basecoat the apple with Barn Red.

2 Using a ½-inch (12mm) angular shader, float Chocolate Cherry on the top of the apple to create the stem end.

Apple

This pattern may be hand-traced or photocopied for personal use only. It is shown here full size.

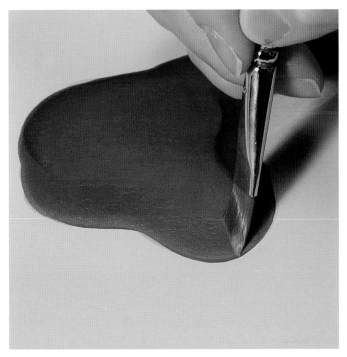

3 Float a little Orange on the side opposite the shading to create a highlight.

4 With a no. 4 flat brush double-loaded with Burnt Umber and Bambi Brown, pull a little stem out from the apple.

5 Add leaves with Dark and Medium Foliage Greens.

Apple Variation

1 Basecoat the apple with Butter Yellow.

2 Using the filbert rake brush and thinned Barn Red, pull up from the apple's bottom end. Paint the streaks following the contours of the apple.

3 Continue to streak the red up the apple until you like the way it looks. Add a few S stroke leaves with Dark and Medium Foliage Greens. Add the blossom end with a little Black loaded on a no. 1 liner brush.

Orange

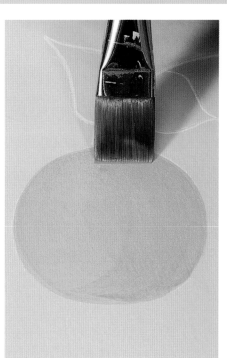

1 Basecoat the orange with Butter Yellow using a no. 10 filbert brush.

2 Add a wash of Bittersweet Orange over the entire orange.

3 With a scruffy brush, or stippler, pat on more Bittersweet Orange. This will add the dimply texture.

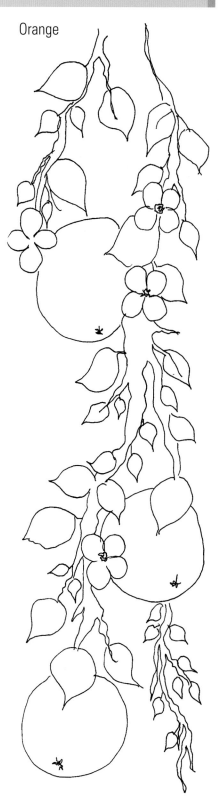

Orange

This pattern may be hand-traced or photocopied for personal use only. Enlarge at 200% to bring up to full size.

4 Add leaves with Dark Foliage Green and Medium Foliage Green double-loaded on a no. 10 filbert brush.

5 Paint the five-petal flower in Oyster White loaded on a no. 10 filbert brush.

6 With a no. 1 liner brush, add the flower center with Bittersweet Orange and Burnt Sienna.

7 Add the stem with Dark Foliage Green.

Grapes

1 Basecoat the stool with Oyster White. Let the sea sponge sit in water for about thirty minutes while the paint dries.

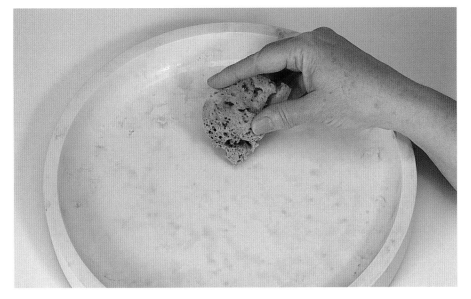

2 Squeeze a sponge full of clean water on your palette. With a very damp sponge, but not dripping wet, pick up Purple Dusk. Sponge lightly on the surface of the stool. Let dry completely.

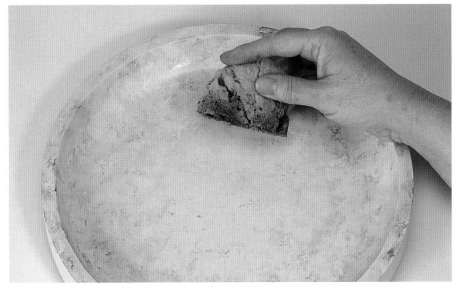

3 Apply Midnight Blue in the same manner, using the same plate and sponge. Sponge lightly, but more toward the edges than in the center. Let this dry completely.

4 Using a sponge, apply paint to the leaf press (or rubber stamp). Use Pine Green and Antique Gold. Apply the Antique Gold randomly on the press (or stamp) as shown.

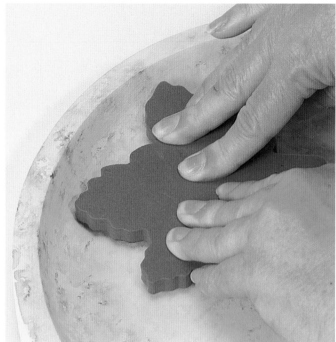

5 Press the stamp onto the surface. Make sure you apply it straight down and with firm pressure. You want to be sure the stamp doesn't slide on the surface.

6 Be sure to lift straight up. Repeat these steps as many times as needed until you're satisfied with the results.

7 Completed grape leaves.

8 Using a stencil dauber loaded with Midnight Blue, paint the back layer of grapes. Apply them randomly in the center.

9 Double-load the stencil dauber with Midnight Blue and Purple Dusk. Pounce on the palette to blend colors.

10 Fill in areas to begin defining the individual grape clusters.

Grapes, continued

11 With the same mix as in the previous step, add a little Butter Cream to the light side of the dauber. Begin adding more grapes with the highlight side toward the outside of the cluster. Add some highlights to the grapes in the previous steps.

12 Double-load Burnt Umber and Pine Green on a no. 1 liner brush. Paint the tendrils. The two colors will create the shading and highlighting.

More Fruit Ideas...

This wonderful grape stool will add a little Old World flavor to your kitchen or den.

Blackberries on a wooden spatula will make a wonderful gift or a decoration for yourself. The spatula can be found just about anywhere making this a quick and inexpensive project.

What a wonderfully fruity kitchen you'll have with a few of these fantastic canisters and spatulas or spoons. In an afternoon, you could decorate your entire kitchen.

Add a little fruit to your floor with this wonderful floorcloth made from a scrap piece of linoleum. Paint the back and your floorcloth won't slip and slide like regular canvas floorcloths. Make sure you apply two coats of Gesso to the backside of the linoleum (the painting side) before you begin to paint.

Add a message to a plaque or message center and send a little love to a special person.

PULL IT ALL TOGETHER

M any years ago when I took my first decorative painting class, I painted daisies. Since that time I have painted daisies in many styles, some very quick and easy and some that seemed to take forever. Finally, I discovered that if I undercoated and painted wet-on-wet, I could get a look I liked and still paint quick daisies. Daisies are so fresh and can be used with almost any fruit or flower to form a pretty design. If you take time to practice, you'll find many uses for daisies in your own designs.

Daisy Basket Lid

This pattern may be hand-traced or photocopied for personal use only. Enlarge at 148% to bring it up to full size.

Materials

Surface
- Round basket from Pesky Bear

Brushes
- nos. 4, 6, 8 filberts
- nos. 0, 1 liner
- All-Purpose brush
- scruffy brush
- ½-inch angular shader
- Sandy's Sure Stroke

Colors
- Glacier Blue
- Cadet Blue
- Midnight Blue
- Walnut
- Magnolia White
- Straw
- Candy Bar Brown
- Black
- Black Green
- Dark Foliage Green
- Medium Foliage Green
- Light Foliage Green
- Old Parchment

Additional Supplies
- Old toothbrush
- Wood Sealer
- Sandpaper
- Tack cloth
- White chalk pencil

Prepare Your Surface

 1 Sand any rough areas on the basket lid.

creative hint:
If a piece is not extremely rough, sand it after it's been sealed. This will save you from doing an extra step.

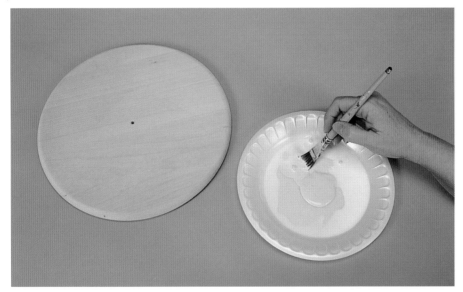

2 Prepare your basecoat by mixing your wood sealer with Old Parchment (1:1).

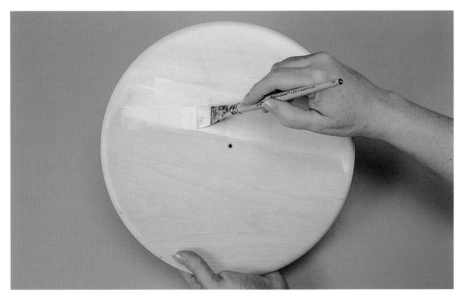

3 Basecoat the surface with the paint and sealer mix. Let the first coat dry thoroughly. Then sand the surface and wipe the dust off with a tack cloth. Apply the second coat. Some colors require a third coat, but Old Parchment covers well in just two.

Paint the Background Foliage

1 Using the All-Purpose brush, pounce in the background foliage. Use all the greens on your palette, starting with the darkest color. The foliage color choices can be found on page 26. You'll need a variety of greens to correspond with the leaves.

2 After the background foliage has dried, transfer the pattern. The ovals represent the size and shape of the daisies and daisy centers. This will help you maintain a good layout for your design and allow you to be spontaneous as well.

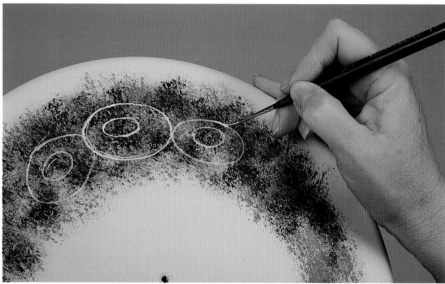

3 Using a no. 8 filbert brush, place a few large leaves around the daisies. These can be one- or two-stroke leaves depending on the room available. The darkest green color is used for the larger leaves.

Paint the Daisies

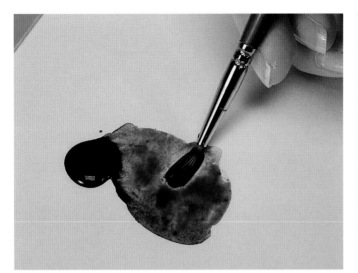

1 Using a round brush (I use Sandy's Sure Stroke, or no. 4 round), thin Dark Foliage Green with water to make a wash, transparent, but not runny. If the paint is too thick, the base stroke daisy petals will be very dark. If the paint is too thin, it will run when you try to paint the petals.

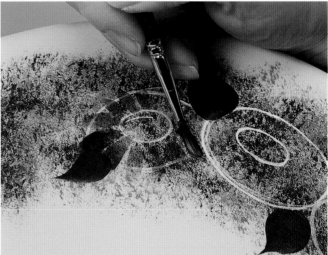

2 When placing your understrokes, you'll need to work quickly, in order to overstoke into the wet paint. Using a comma stroke, paint the understroke, starting at the outside circle and stroking toward the inner circle. These strokes will be covered up with Magnolia White later.

3 Begin the daisy petals by painting the two side front petals first and work toward center front. The petals on the sides should be curved toward the center of the flower. The strokes should get longer and straighter closer to the front. Then, paint the side petals and work toward the back. The back petals get shorter as they get closer to back center. You can vary the number of petals a daisy has. It simply depends on the size of the daisy, the size of the brush, and the amount of pressure you apply when making the strokes.

4 Let your daisy petals dry before proceeding.

Paint the Daisy Center

1 With your round brush, pat a basecoat of Straw in the center of each daisy. Let this dry.

2 Using an old scruffy brush, double-load the brush with Straw and Candy Bar Brown. Then, pat the end of the bristles on your palette to blend. Starting with the Candy Bar Brown side at the back edge of the daisy center, pat the shading around the left side, walking the colors in toward the center and out. This will help blend the colors. Let this dry.

3 Using the old scruffy brush loaded with a little bit of Magnolia White, pat in a highlight on the right side of center. This gives you a little hint of a highlight.

4 Using the bristle end of a no. 1 liner brush tipped in Black, make dots randomly around the outside edge of the daisy center. You can add a few dots using other colors from your design to add a little variety.

The completed daisies.

Paint the Branches

1 Using a no. 1 liner brush loaded with Black on one side and Walnut on the other, randomly place your branches with a wiggly stroke. Apply a varied amount of pressure to your brush to get a variety of branch sizes.

2 With a white chalk pencil, place the blueberries randomly throughout the design in clusters of three.

Paint the Berries

1 Basecoat the blueberries using a no. 4 filbert brush loaded with Cadet Blue.

2 Shade the blueberries using a ½-inch (12mm) angular shader. Float Midnight Blue on the bottom of the berries and where they're underneath another berry.

3 Highlight the blueberries with a ½-inch (12mm) angular shader. Float Glacier Blue in the upper left corner to indicate a highlight.

4 Place a small dot for the blossom end of the blueberry using a no. 1 liner brush loaded with Black. Then, paint small wispy lines going away from the center to form a star shape. This is the actual blossom.

Paint the Filler Flowers

1 Paint the filler flowers using Glacier Blue and the no. 4 filbert brush. Make filler flowers by placing the brush down flat and twisting onto the side edge, pulling slightly toward the center to form a point on each of the petals. I usually make four to five petals for each flower.

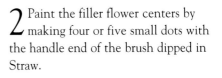

2 Paint the filler flower centers by making four or five small dots with the handle end of the brush dipped in Straw.

3 Shade the filler flower centers with the handle end of the brush dipped into Candy Bar Brown. Add 1 or 2 dots quickly after the first coat, so you're painting wet-into-wet.

Finishing Touches

1 Paint the tendrils using a no. 0 liner brush loaded with Dark Foliage Green.

2 Using a stiff-bristled brush or toothbrush and Midnight Blue thinned with water, spatter in the basecoat areas. You can do the flyspecking before or after you have completed the painting.

3 Paint little filler leaves on the handle with the same greens you used on the basket lid using a no. 4 filbert brush.

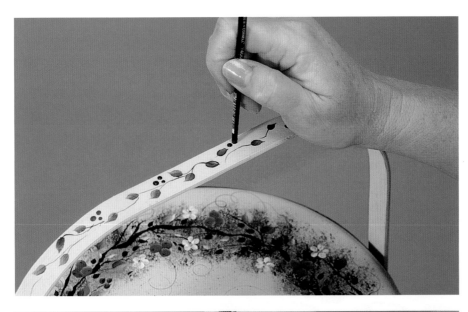

4 Add blueberries to the basket handle using the same brush's handle dipped in Midnight Blue. Randomly, make the dots in sets of three.

5 Using Dark Foliage Green and a no. 1 liner brush, connect the leaves and dots on the handle with vines and stems. Using a variety of filbert brush sizes (4-6-8), begin filling in the design with leaves painted Black Green, Dark Foliage Green, Medium Foliage Green, Light Foliage Green and Glacier Blue. Add interest to your design by using any combination of these colors double-loaded on your brush to create a variety of filler leaves.

More Daisy Ideas...

The completed daisy basket

Combine daisies, leaves and fruit for striking combinations.

DESIGN YOUR OWN

You Can Do It!

So, you've always wanted to design your own pieces, but it always seemed too intimidating? Here is how I combine fruit with flowers and pick colors. Before you know it, you'll be painting your own quick and easy originals.

Let's Doodle...

When you're trying to put a project together, sit down with a pencil and a blank sheet of paper and just doodle. Start by making a rough sketch of the surface. (When I say rough, I mean rough. I still find it difficult to draw things accurately.)

Place a basket or container in the design first. Then put in the focal flowers. These can just be large ovals or circles if you like. Decide where you are going to need filler and what you would like to see there—maybe a color or maybe a flower or leaf. Just draw a blob or a triangle to hold that place. Use simple shapes to lay out your design.

I use a chalk pencil to help me keep these smaller items as well as fruits and berries to the correct size. If I don't do this, I tend to make my blueberries or raspberries bigger than the focal flowers.

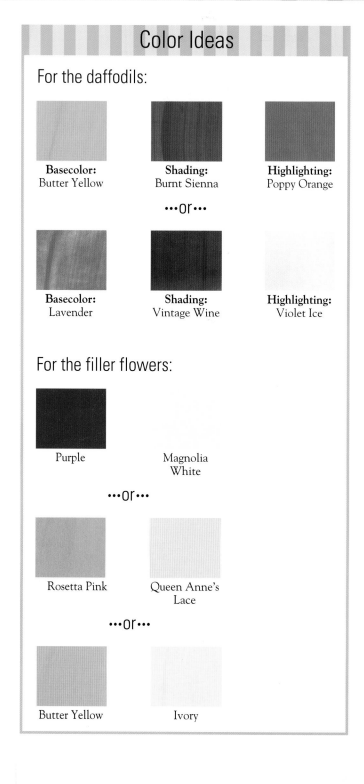

Color Ideas

For the daffodils:

Basecolor:
Butter Yellow

Shading:
Burnt Sienna

Highlighting:
Poppy Orange

···or···

Basecolor:
Lavender

Shading:
Vintage Wine

Highlighting:
Violet Ice

For the filler flowers:

Purple

Magnolia White

···or···

Rosetta Pink

Queen Anne's Lace

···or···

Butter Yellow

Ivory

Refine Your Design

Once you're pretty happy with your general design, go back and refine it. Make the circles, ovals and triangles look a little more like flowers or fruit. You still don't have to draw the filler leaves or flowers. Perhaps you would feel more comfortable drawing the flowers to the side.

Add the Color

Okay, so you made it through the drawing part, now what? It's time to choose the colors. This is one of the most fun areas of designing your own pieces.

This is easy. Choose the colors you like. I prefer deep, rich colors, but if you prefer pastels, go with it. Remember you can change any of the flower colors in this book to match your decor or your preference.

I'm always asked questions in classes about the shading and highlighting colors. This has been made easy by the major paint manufacturers. They can provide a shading and highlighting guide that lists every color in their line and what the shading and highlighting colors are for your favorite colors.

Don't forget you can visit your local department store to stare at their towels and linens to get color ideas. They know the latest trends in home decorating, so use their expertise.

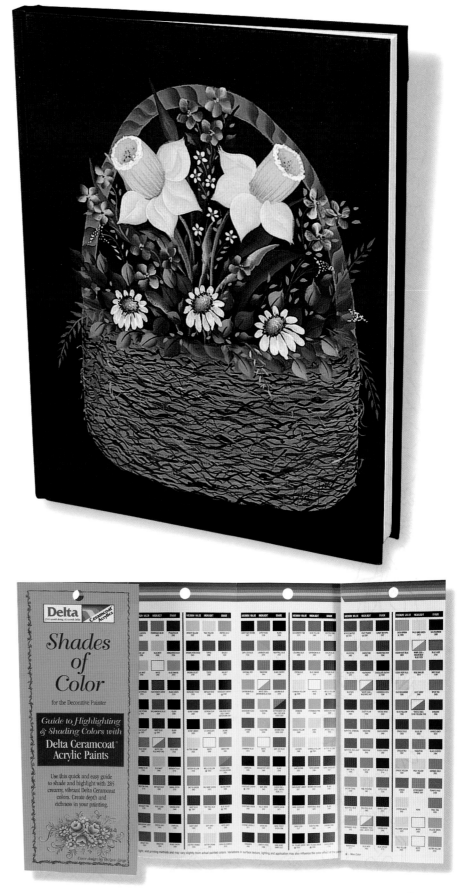

You can get this brochure by writing to Delta Technical Coatings; 2550 Pellissier Place; Whittier, CA 90601 or call 1-800-423-4135. Their web address is www.deltacrafts.com.

Pattern for Cover Art

This pattern may be hand-traced or photocopied for personal use only. Enlarge at 128% to bring it up to full size.

Resource List

Products

Eagle Brush, Inc. - Brushes
431 Commerce Park Drive SE
Suite 100&101
Marietta, Georgia 30060
770-419-4855
800-832-4532

Loew-Cornell, Inc. - Brushes
563 Chestnut Ave.
Teaneck, NJ 07666-2490
201-836-7070
web site: www.loew-cornell.com
E-mail: loew-cornell@loew-cornell.com

In Argentina:
Cleo International Especials
Arenales 2532 (1425)
Buenos Aires, Argentina
54-1148242009

In Australia:
Bauernmalerei Folk & Dec. Art
P. O. Box 616
Narrabeen Australia NSW 2101
61-2-9979422

In Brazil:
Arte Versata
Sep/Sul-Eq 705/905-Bloco C
Centro Empresarial Mont Blanc
Brazilia/DF 70.390-055

In Japan:
Dean's Inc
M-1 Bldg 2F
1-1-4 Nigashi Nihonbashi Chuo-ku
Tokyo, Japan
81-3-3861-2555

Royal Brush Manufacturing, Inc.
6707 Broadway
Merrillville, IN 46410
219-660-4170

Daler-Rowney/Robert Simmons
2 Corporate Dr.
Canbury, NJ 08512-9584
609-655-5252

Delta Technical Coatings, Inc. -
Delta Ceramcoat Acrylic Paint
2550 Pellissier Place
Whittier, California 90601
562-695-7969

J.W. Etc. - Prep and Finishing
Products
2205 First Street #103
Simi Valley, California 93065
805-526-5066

Walnut Hollow - Memory Album
Cover #3703
1409 State Road 23
Dodgeville, Wisconsin 53533-2112
608-935-2341

Pesky Bear
5059 Roszyk Hill Road
Machias, New York 14101
Phone/fax 716-942-3250

Index